Easy Techniques for Creating Stunning Wire Jewelry

Natalie M. Hayes

Funny helpful tips:

Learn the art of compromise; relationships thrive on mutual understanding and flexibility.

Harness the power of big data; its analysis is driving business strategies, research, and decision-making.

Easy Techniques for Creating Stunning Wire Jewelry : Unlock Your Creativity and Master the Art of Crafting Exquisite Wire Jewelry Effortlessly

Life advices:

Limit saturated and trans fats; they can lead to cardiovascular issues and weight gain.

Engage with voice-activated assistants; they're simplifying tasks and offering hands-free device interactions.

Introduction

This is your comprehensive step-by-step guide to embarking on a creative journey with wire and crafting stunning jewelry pieces. This guide equips you with the knowledge and skills needed to create unique wire jewelry projects, from necklaces and bracelets to rings, earrings, and even anklets.

The introduction sets the stage for your wire jewelry-making adventure, highlighting the reasons why working with wire is a rewarding and creative endeavor.

The guide then delves into specific jewelry projects, starting with DIY wire necklace projects. These projects are not only creative but also allow you to explore your unique style.

Following that, you'll discover eye-catching wire bracelet projects that enable you to craft stunning wristwear, perfect for adding a personal touch to your outfits.

Elegance takes center stage with wire ring jewelry projects. You'll learn to create beautiful wire rings that can serve as meaningful gifts or statement pieces for your own collection.

For those who adore earrings, the guide offers amazing wire earring projects, each with its own charm and style.

To adorn your ankles, there are dazzling wire anklet jewelry projects that provide step-by-step instructions for crafting jewelry that's perfect for warmer seasons.

The guide concludes with a super detailed section, offering expert guidance on how to make your own wire jewelry efficiently.

It then delves into the essential aspects of working with wire jewelry, including how to get started and the key skills you'll need to develop.

The guide provides insights into producing various types of jewelry, such as earrings, bracelets, and necklaces, ensuring you're well-equipped to create a wide range of wire jewelry pieces.

This book is the ideal resource for anyone interested in the art of crafting wire jewelry. Whether you're a novice or an experienced jewelry maker, this guide empowers you to unleash your creativity and create stunning wire jewelry pieces that reflect your personal style and flair.

Contents

Wire Jewelry

Step-by-Step Guide To Begin Your Wire Journey and Create Amazing Jewelry Yourself

Introduction: Why You Should Work with Wood

Since I was a child I have always wanted to learn how to create my own jewelry but most of the time I was frustrated because I wasn't able to create them properly. So I took a lot of time practicing and studying how to create pieces of jewelry the right way and I learned that beginners like us must know how to utilize various materials such as wires before you progress into a much complicated ones such as using materials that are very difficult to mold.

This is where I learned that with the use of wire you can create astounding pieces of jewelry and its advantage the other materials used in creating jewelry is that it is super easy to mold. This is where I got an idea to master the craft of creating pieces of jewelry with the use of a wire. Luckily, I have adapted the knowledge very well which led me in creating promising projects and in this book I have the privilege to impart my knowledge to you on how to make satisfying wire jewelry projects.

Chapter 1 – Creative DIY Wire Necklace Jewelry Projects

Ever dream of having those beautiful necklaces you always see in the malls? But kind of sad because most of them are very expensive. Believe it or not, you can make these necklaces right into your own home. The good thing about these DIY necklaces is that they are not expensive, you just need some basic materials in order to start making this fancy necklace, like copper wires, beads, and some pliers.

For a cheap amount of materials, you can now own a necklace as beautiful as or more beautiful than the ones in the mall. So what are we waiting for? Let's start making these nice and beautiful necklaces. Make sure to follow every step.

Wire Wrapped Pendant – this wire wrapped pendants will surely make the people around you look at you and be amazed because of the attracting features your DIY pendant has. This pendant is not that hard to make so suit up and let's make this right away.

The materials that you need:

1 small cabochon stone

3 pieces of 21 or 20 gauge square dead soft copper wire (about 7 inches each piece)

22 gauge half round dead soft copper wire (no need to measure, just keep on the spool and use as needed)

Pliers

Round nose pliers

Wire Cutters

String or small metal chain (for the pendant)

Step 1: Grab your 3 pieces of copper wire and the cabochon stone. Shape the wires depending on the size of the stone you have. Make sure that it is equally measured.

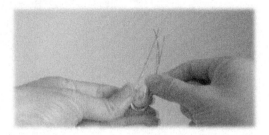

Step2: Remove the stone and tighten up the shaped wire.

Step 3: Grab enough length of your soft wire. Make sure that it can wrap over the middle of the shaped wire.

Step 4: Wrap around the soft wire on the middle of the shaped wire. Then cut the ends.

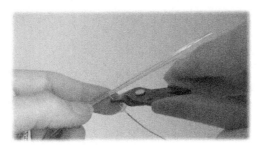

Step 5: With the use of round nose pliers, flatten up the soft wire you've wrapped around on the middle of the shaped-wire.

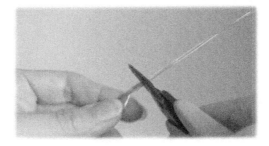

Step 6: Grab your cabochon stone again and shape the wire around it.

Step 7: Remove the cabochon stone. And with the use of round nose pliers, bend out even further both sides of the bent wire.

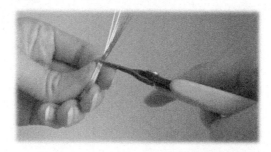

Step 8: Grab another soft wire and then wrap it around the middle of the bent shaped wire.

Step 9: After wrapping it around, bring down two wires of both sides on the three pieces of wire you have.

Step 10: Grab a long piece of your soft wire and then wrap it around the remaining two thick wires.

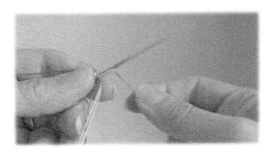

Step 11: After reaching the middle of the wires while wrapping, cut the end of the soft wire.

Step 12: After cutting the end, grab your round nose pliers and flatten out the wrapped soft wire.

Step 13: Again with the use of your round nose pliers, pinch the end of the wrapped soft wire and then bend it.

Step 14: Bend the wire with the wrapped soft wire around your finger.

Step 15: Bend the recently bent wire even tighter to become small.

Step 16: Unravel the recently wrapped around the wire on the middle of the shaped wire.

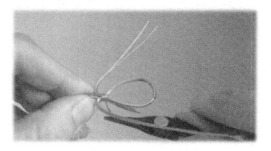

Step 17: Wrap this unraveled wire around the middle again but together with the recently bent wire in order to connect them.

Step 18: after wrapping it around, grab your pliers and then cut the ends.

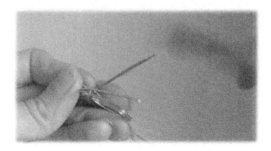

Step 19: Using your round nose pliers, flatten the wrapped wire.

Step 20: Bring back your cabochon stone on the wire. Fit it tightly.

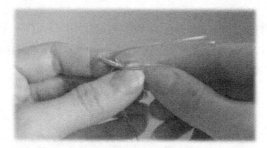

Step 21: This is where things will get different. Using the remaining wires spread out, tightly secure the cabochon stone so that it won't fall off. You can shape this wire in any design you want. It may not look the same as in the picture because it will depend on the size of the cabochon stone you use and the design of wire you'll be doing.

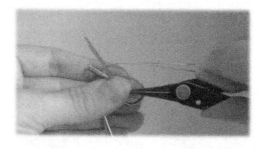

Step 22: You can now put this pendant on any string or metal chain of your choice to have your beautiful and dazzling necklace. Now that you've finished this beautiful necklace, it is now up to you if you're going to make this as your own jewelry or can wrap it and make it as a gift for a loved one. Enjoy your DIY necklace!

Simple Star Necklace – a very cute star designed-wire necklace. I'm very sure that after making this necklace, you'll be easily noticed by the people around you as you can spark up like the star while wearing this one. So how do we make this necklace? Let's find out and follow the steps carefully.

The materials that you need:

20 gauge copper wire (12 cm or depends on how big you want to create your star)

Pliers

Cutting Pliers

Marker

Ruler

Damp cloth

A string of your choice

Step 1: Make sure that the wire you'll be using is straight. Now grab your ruler and marker. Equally, divide the wire into 5 parts and mark it with a marker.

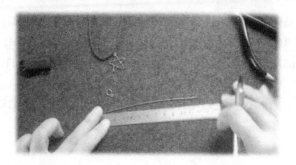

Step 2: After marking the wires, carefully twist and bend these marked areas and create a star.

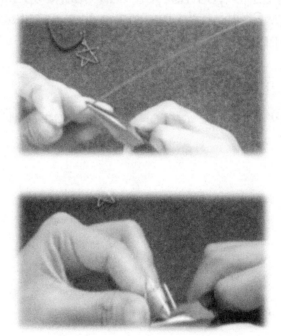

Step 4: After making the star shape out of the wire, cut the one end and leave one end to make the hook.

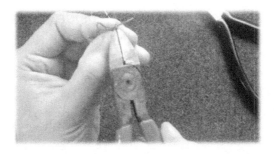

Step 5: For the other end that you didn't cut, start bending it to make the hook.

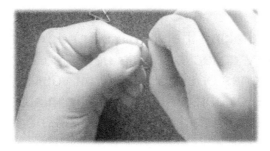

Step 6: Using a damp cloth, clean the star-shaped wire.

Step 7: After cleaning up the star-shaped wire, tighten up each side of the star.

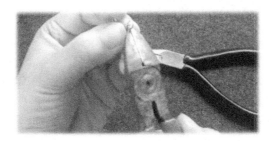

Step 8: Insert the string of your choice inside the hook. Now, you are done making your own star-shaped wire necklace.

We are now done making the simple star necklace. You can add this to your DIY jewelry collection. This necklace can also be a simple gift for your loved ones or simply show off your style by wearing this. If you are the type of person that is really interested in making this kind of jewelry, you can start a business from here.

Chapter 2 – Eye-Catchy DIY Wire Bracelet Jewelry Projects

Known for its popularity in the fashion industry, bracelets are one of the most notable things a person can where. From dazzling jewelry designs to simplistic string-made bracelets, these things will bring out the artistic and stylish side of you. But wait, finding it hard to provide yourself a bracelet, the type of bracelet that can make the people around look at you and say: "I also want that bracelet, it is very beautiful." Luckily, you can make these bracelets right in your house.

All you need is a couple of copper wires, some beads, and pliers. Simple right? So what are you waiting for? Stay tuned as I list down some of the best DIY wire bracelets. Follow each step carefully.

Shiny Beads Style Bracelet – an outstanding bracelet you can confidently bring out with you, whether you are going shopping at the mall or attending an important family event, this bracelet is just perfect. Just by looking at it, you wouldn't know that it is only homemade. Can you believe that?! Now let's start this fancy bracelet.

The materials that you need:

1mm round wire (18 gauge)

0.4mm round wire (26 gauge)

Beads (size and color depends on you)

Pliers

Cutting pliers

Step 1: Grab 50 cm of 1mm round wire (thick wire) and straighten it out.

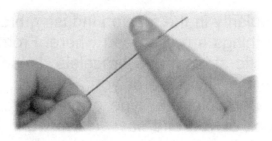

Step 2: Using your pliers, bend at least 10 cm of the thick wire.

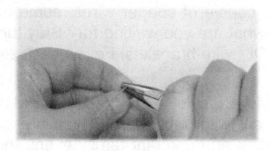

Step 3: Pinch and tighten the bent wire.

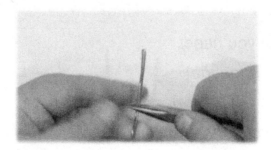

Step 4: Bend a quarter of the bottom end of the bent wire.

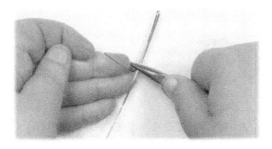

Step 5: Wrap that bent quarter around the wire itself.

Step 6: For the remaining wire out of that wrapped part, make swirl and flatten it.

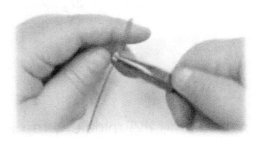

Step 7: Grab a very long size (3 pieces) of the 0.4 mm round wire (thin wire).

Step 8: Find the middle of the thin wire by connecting the endpoints.

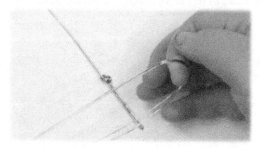

Step 9: Once you have found the middle, wrap it crossover the top of the swirled wire on the thick wire.

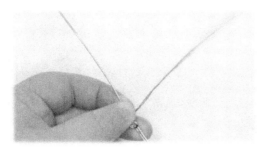

Step 10: Get one bead and then insert it in the thick wire.

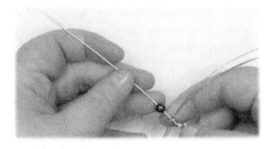

Step 11: Grab the right side of the thin wires (the ones wrapped over the thick wire) and then wrap it across the top of the bead. Repeat it on the left side of the thin wire.

Step 12: After doing this crossover pattern, grab another bead and then insert it in the thick wire.

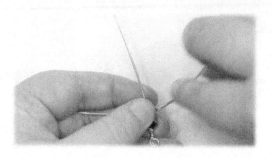

<u>Step 13:</u> Then repeat step 11 until all your beads are inserted on the thick wire, or until you have reached your desired bracelet length.

<u>Step 14:</u> Now secure the end of the bracelet. To do this, grab one piece of the extended thin wire and wrap it two times on the thick wire over on the opposite side (if the wires are on the right side, you are going to wrap it to the left side and plus, wrap it inwards).

Step 15: As you can see, on both left and right you have 3 extended wires on each. If you started on the right side, continue step 14 until the wires on the right side are completely wrapped on the thick wire. If you started left side, it is still the same.

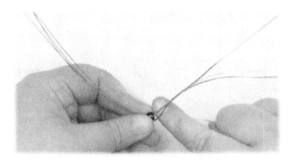

Step 16: Now finish it with the other side of the extended wire. After wrapping them all, cut off the excess wires and flatten the sharp points with your pliers to prevent it from scraping your skin.

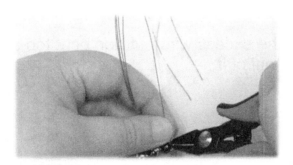

Step 17: Using your pliers, pinch the end of the thick wire and start making a loop (this is where you are going to insert the hook to secure the bracelet).

Step 18: Twist the excess part of the thick wire around itself to secure the loop created.

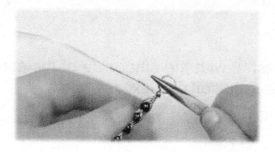

Step 19: Cut off the excess wire but don't cut too short, leave some and make a swirl out of it.

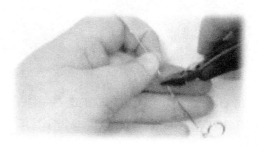

Step 20: Flatten out the swirl created to match the bracelet perfectly.

Step 21: Back to the other end of the bracelet, bend it out and shape it like a hook.

Step 22: Slowly bring the bracelet together, and shape it evenly.

Step 23: Now you can attach the hook on the loop and style out with this dazzling Shiny Beads Style Bracelet.

Simple Patterned Wire Bracelet – this simplistic bracelet is just perfect for any event or activity you are going to. This bracelet is highly customizable and adjustable based on your wrist's size and based on the artistic side of you. This bracelet is also for men and women, so all in all, it is just the best and easy DIY wire bracelet you can have! So let's get started.

The materials that you need:

Thick copper wires

Thin copper wires

Round nose pliers

Pliers

Cutting pliers

Bottle (for mold)

Step 1: Grab a long piece of your thick wire and straighten it out.

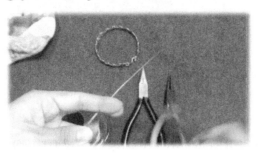

Step 2: Cut two pieces of the thick wire (same length depending on the size you want to make).

Step 3: Get one of that thick wire and then make this bend.

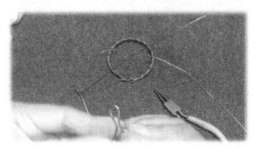

Step 4: Get a long piece of thin wire and find its middle by connecting both ends of it. Then right after, wrap the thin wire around the neck of the bend on the thick wire you have just made.

Step 5: Get the second thick wire and make the same bend as the first one.

Step 6: Insert this bend or loop over the first thick wire.

Step 7: Grab the thin wire and wrap it around the inserted thick wire.

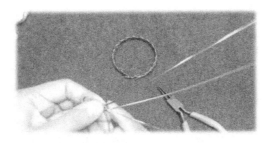

Step 8: After wrapping it, make the same bend like the recent ones on the excess of the thick wires itself.

Step 9: Then repeat step 7 and 8 over and over until you have reached your desired length.

Step 10: Cut off the excess wires but leave some of the thick wires (you will use it as hooks).

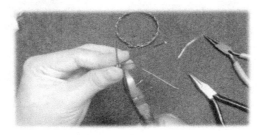

Step 11: From the remaining thick wires, bend it to create a hook. Flatten out with your round nose pliers to prevent scraping the skin.

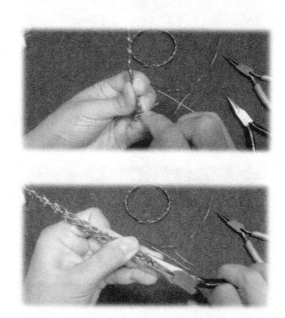

Step 12: Slowly bring each end to each other and then put the hook on the end loop.

Chapter 3 – Elegant Wire Ring Jewelry Projects

Have a different style? Like choosing a ring over bracelet and necklaces, well, we all know that rings are not that affordable (the ones with the high quality), but whenever it is affordable, we also know that it will not last long because it is made up of cheap materials that break easily.

But do you know that you can make high-quality rings in your home? Yes, you heard that right! Just a couple of copper wires and your handy pliers, you are good to go. You can make cool rings that can easily attract anyone. These rings are guaranteed high quality in looks and sturdy in build. Now let's make these cool rings.

Shiny Bead Ring – with this shiny bead ring, you'll definitely reach the level of those models that advertises ring jewelry or better, you can beat them in level. Just made of some beads and sturdy copper wire, you can now have a high-quality ring.

The materials that you need:

Thick copper wires

Thin copper wires

Ring mandrel

Cutting pliers

Round nose pliers

4 Small beads

Step 1: Grab a long piece of thick wire and insert the four small beads in the thick copper wire.

Step 2: Bring all the beads in the middle of the thick wire.

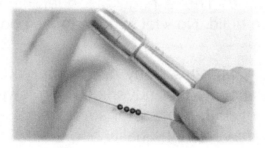

Step 3: Measure the size of the ring using the ring mandrel. Make sure to have spaces on the beads as you make the circular shape.

Step 4: After getting the size of your ring, wrap around both sides of the thick wire just to lock up the shape temporarily.

Step 5: Remove the ring from the ring mandrel.

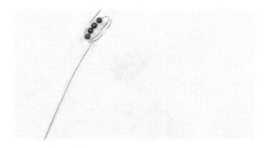

Step 6: Get a long piece of the thin wire and then start by wrapping one side of the thick wire inwards to the other side.

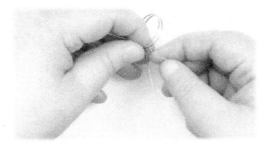

Step 7: Continue to do this pattern until you reach the end of the other ring.

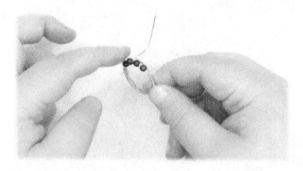

Step 8: Grab your cutting pliers and then cut off the excess wire.

Step 9: Gently bend the excess wire from the thick wire.

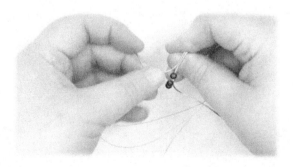

Step 10: Grab 3 long pieces of thin copper wire, find its middle by connecting both ends. Once you've found the middle point, wrap it around at one end of the ring with the recently bent excess part of the thick wire.

Step 11: After wrapping it around, flatten the three thin copper wires. Start at the right side of the thin copper wires and bend it over the bead while securing it on the next space of the next bead. Do this same pattern on the left side of the thin wires until you reach the end of the four beads.

Step 12: Once you have reached the end of the beads. Start again on the right side of the thin wires, grab one wire and then wrap it over the space right at the end of the last bead, then follow it up with the next wire up to the third one. Do the same thing on the left side of the thin wires.

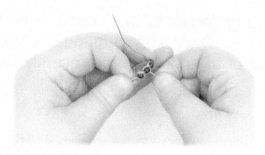

<u>Step 13:</u> Once you've done it, grab your pliers and cut off the excess thin copper wires.

<u>Step 14:</u> With the use of your round nose pliers, flatten the edges of the wires to prevent it from scraping your skin.

<u>Step 15:</u> Now you are almost done. The next thing to do is grab one excess wire from the thick wires and then wrap it over the space before the bead. Do this same thing to the other excess wire of the thick copper wire.

<u>Step 16:</u> Using your cutting pliers, cut off the excess wires.

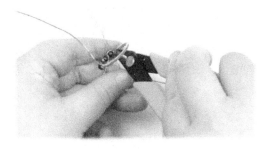

<u>Step 17:</u> Grab you, round nose pliers, again and then flatten each end of the wires to make it smooth.

<u>Step 18:</u> Check if it is still sharp.

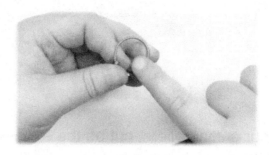

<u>Step 19:</u> If it is still sharp, flatten it again with your round nose pliers.

Now you have your Shiny Bead Ring. You can now stand out in the fashion trend with this cool and eye-catching ring. It can also be a perfect gift for a friend or relative!

Simple Cabochon Stone Ring – want to buy a ring with a precious stone on it but can't afford it because it is too expensive? Don't worry, I got you! With this simple ring, you can have your own version of the precious stone ring. The things you'll be needing will not cost you that much so it's a win-win on your budget and on your fashion statement. So what are we waiting for? Let's dive through in making this gorgeous ring.

The materials that you need:

Cabochon stone (spaced out on the sides)

Long thick copper wires

Round nose pliers

Cutting pliers

Ring mandrel

Step 1: Grab your cabochon stone (we will be using cabochon stones with spaces on the sides to easily hold the wires).

Step 2: Cut a long piece on your thick copper wire, find its middle by connecting the two endpoints of the wire. After finding its middle, wrap it around the side of the cabochon stone.

Step 3: Twist the wire using your round nose pliers to secure the cabochon stone in place.

Step 4: Grab your ring mandrel and then measure the size of the ring you want. Put the ring in place and bend over the wire to the desired ring size.

Step 5: After finding your desired size, remove the ring from the mandrel. Grab one end of the thick wire and start making a swirl or a

design that you prefer.

Step 6: Do the same thing on the other end of the copper wire.

Step 7: Try out the ring if it fits exactly on your fingers. If it fits in then you're all set.

Now that you've finished this wonderful ring, you can now show this off in public, whether you are going to the mall or just walk in your local park. Remember that this ring is highly customizable, so anytime you can unravel it and change the way it looks or just simply adjust the size.

Chapter 4 – Amazing Wire Earrings Jewelry Projects

Earrings are part of the fashion industry a very long time ago. Based on a study, earrings are already in existence since the Ancient Egyptians, Dang! That was a very long time ago indeed. But are you curious why it is still trendy up to this day? Although in the market there are a lot of expensive earrings, imitations come in the place that is why a lot of people have access to these things. But of course, you don't like this limitation, because most of them cost almost the same as the expensive ones but don't last that long. A waste of money right?

But do you know that you can invest in something that you can make right in your own place for an affordable price, but high in quality the same as the expensive ones? Yes, that's right! Today I'll guide you on different steps on how to make your own earrings just by using a piece of wire. Let's get started.

Simple Rose Earrings – this rose earrings will bring out the best in you. It comes with a vibrant color because of the copper wire used, plus it is easy to make and guaranteed can give you that outstanding look in the public.

The materials that you need:

Thick copper wires

Circular mold

Cutting pliers

Pliers

Nail file

Step 1: Grab a piece of your thick copper wire (depends on how long enough you want to use).

Step 2: Grab your circular mold and then wrap around the thick copper wire on it. (Make sure you start to wrap around in the middle.)

Step 3: Twist the wire and from the middle point the twist created, circle around one part of the thick wire.

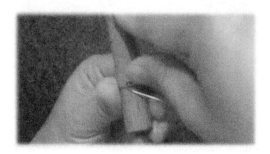

Step 4: Continue this circle with the other part of the thick copper wire (this will make the rose shape).

Step 5: After making a rose shape, cut one end of the excess wire and leave the other wire long.

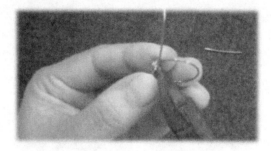

Step 6: Flatten the edge of the wire you've just cut.

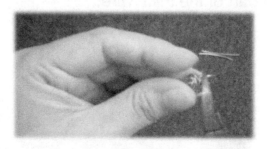

Step 7: Straighten the long end of the wire.

Step 8: Using a nail file, polish the end of the long thick copper wire to prevent scraping the skin.

Now your rose earrings are all set up. You can now confidently walk on the streets with this simple but stylish earrings.

Shiny Beads Earrings – this another earring will surely fit in your fashion taste. It comes with a simplistic bead earring design and a sturdy structure supported by a thick copper wire, now you don't have to worry for the beads that might fall off your ears. So what are we waiting for? Let's start making this amazing earring.

The materials that you need:

Two beads

Cutting pliers

Pliers

Round nose pliers

Thick copper wires

Nail file

Circular mold

<u>Step 1:</u> Cut two short pieces of wire from your thick copper wire. And make two small knobs on each end.

<u>Step 2:</u> Polish the end using a nail file.

Step 3: With your circular mold, wrap around the two short wires and shape them to create a hook.

Step 4: Cut out a long piece on your thick copper wires.

Step 5: Bend the long piece of copper wire (bend it equally where both ends will meet).

Step 6: Cut this bent long piece in the middle. Grab one piece of the wire and set aside the other one.

Step 7: On the one piece of wire you have, grab your pliers and twist the end to make a little knob.

Step 8: Insert one bead on the wire.

Step 9: As you can see that little knob you created keeps the bead in place. Now grab your round nose pliers and start bending the long part of the wire, wrap it around the bead.

Step 10: When you already wrapped the bead with the wire, secure it in the little knob you recently created.

Step 11: Twist it on the knob until the long wire becomes short. Cut off the excess wire.

<u>Step 12:</u> Attach the hooks to the small knobs of the earrings.

Now your all new shiny bead earrings are all set. Be ready for the people who are going to ask you where you bought that cool earring. I am very sure that they will be definitely shocked if you tell them that you made those earrings by yourself.

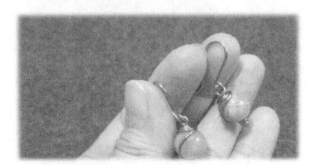

Simple and Easy Heart Earrings – feeling in love? Or simply want to have cute yet catchy earrings? Well, this next earring design is for you. You'll definitely love this heart earrings because they are very easy to make and all you need to have is some piece of wire and your handy pliers. So let's get started.

The materials that you need:

Stud earrings clasps

Silver wires or copper wires

Cutting pliers

Pliers

Round nose pliers

Nail file

Step 1: Starting off with this tutorial, you'll be needing a long silver or copper wire. Cut a long piece and then bend the end to shape the first side of the heart shape.

Step 2: Bend it to the front and from the other side of the wire, make the same shape you've recently made on the other side.

Step 3: Now that you have formed the heart shape from the wire. Cut it off from the long wire (leave enough length where you will put the stud earrings) and polish it with a nail file to prevent scraping the skin.

Now your heart-shaped earrings are ready. You can either use it for personal purposes or make it as a gift for a friend or loved one. All in all, it is not that hard to make right? In just a matter of minutes, you can now have earrings that can match those you can see at the malls. I hope glad that you came here up to this point so far. Now we're close to the last chapter and we'll be discussing DIY anklets, so stay tuned for this last jewelry design.

Chapter 5 – Dazzling Wire Anklet Jewelry Projects

Anklets are like bracelets the only thing that is different is you put the anklet right on your ankle, hence the name. Anklets have been around the world a long time ago, they were worn by women in Ancient Egypt. And I believe that until now, the fashion trend for anklets are still up because they look cool and the same way rare. I guess that you also like to be noticed by wearing an anklet, but don't worry, you don't need to buy one because I am going to teach you on how to make on your own. Stay tuned for this last jewelry design.

Simple Shiny Beads Anklet– this simplistic anklet will surely standout in every situation, whether it is a formal or a casual event. It comes with shiny beads attach to well-design and built copper wires which guarantee its durability.

The materials you need:

Small beads

Thick copper wires

Thin copper wires

Round nose pliers

Pliers

Cutting pliers

Nail file

Step 1: Cut three 10cm thick copper wires.

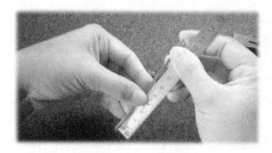

Step 2: Bend the 3 wires and make this shape:

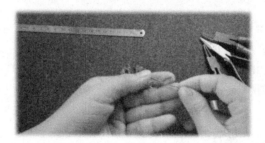

Step 3: Then on one end of the bent wire, make swirl then flatten it together with the wire.

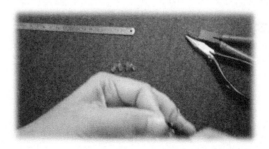

Step 4: Cut one short piece of copper wire and make this shape:

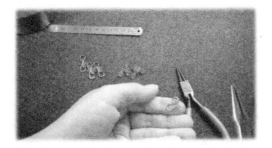

Step 5: Cut off 3 short pieces of copper wire then with the use of your pliers bend the 3 short wires to this shape:

Step 6: Cut 6 short pieces of thick copper wire, using your round nose pliers, make a small loop at the end of each short wire (this will lock the beads in place). Right after making the small loop, insert beads on each wire then using your round nose pliers, secure the ending with a small loop.

Step 7: Grab a long thin copper wire and make a small loop on its end. After making the small loop, insert one bead. Secure it by wrapping over the rest of the wire on the bead and then wrap it around the small loop created.

Step 8: Cut off the excess thin wire and secure it by making a small loop again.

Step 9: The pieces should look like these:

Step 10: Now grab your pliers and start inserting the beads on the 3 wires you've bent on step 2.

<u>Step 11:</u> Continue step 10 while following the arrangement of the beads and wires pictured on step 9.

<u>Step 12:</u> Once you are done connecting the pieces on each other, grab your cutting pliers and then cut the excess wires. With the use of a nail file, polish the end where you cut the excess wires to prevent scarping the skin. Now you are done making your own simple shiny beads anklet. Remember that this anklet is highly adjustable and customizable, so there is no need to worry whenever you change your style in fashion. Now try this astonishing and dazzling anklet!

Two Beads Anklet – this is a simple and easy to make anklet, it only requires you to have a long copper wire or silver wire, some beads, and your trusty pliers. This anklet comes with a vibrant and shiny color which I am sure you'll love and all the people around you who can see it. Now let's start making this anklet!

The materials that you need:

Long copper or silver wire

Beads (2 pieces will do)

Cutting pliers

Round nose pliers

Round object (for shaping the anklet)

Superglue

Step 1: Prepare all the materials you need.

Step 2: Insert one bead in the long copper or silver wire.

Step 3: After inserting the bead in the wire, grab your round nose pliers and make a loop right where you've inserted the bead (this will keep the bead in place.

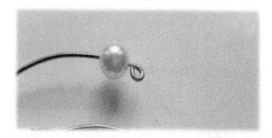

Step 4: Wrap the wire around your preferred round object, or much better, measure it right away on your ankles.

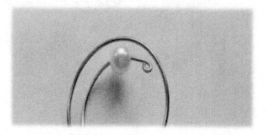

Step 5: After finding the right length or size of your anklet, cut the wire from the other end. Grab another bead and insert it on the other end.

<u>Step 6:</u> Using your round nose pliers, secure the end of the wire by making another small loop to lock the bead in place. Use a superglue and the glue the holes of the beads in place to prevent it from moving around the anklet once you wear it.

Now you are done making this simple and easy anklet. This anklet is also adjustable based on the size of your ankles. With its elegant and pure design, it is perfect for formal events and as gifts for weddings and anniversaries.

***Leaf Shaped Wire Anklet**–* another one simple and easy to make anklet. This anklet comes with a leaf pattern design which will give you the feel of a Greek goddess. Now let's start making this cute and simple anklet!

The materials that you need:

Long nose pliers

One long copper or silver wire

Step 1: Make sure that the copper wire you have is straight. Now using your long nose pliers, make a loop at the end of the wire.

Step 2: From the very end of the loop, pinch it with your long nose pliers and then start bending it downwards.

Step 3: Using your hands, bend the wire to the opposite direction.

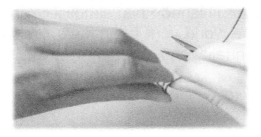

Step 4: Continue doing this pattern downwards the entire wire.

Step 5: Once that you've reached the end of the wire, make a hook from the end (you'll use this hook to attach it on the loop you've created on the other end of the wire).

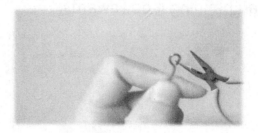

Step 6: Now slowly wrap around the anklet on your ankle to shape it circularly.

Step 7: When you are now satisfied with the size, you can now use it. Now that you've finished this simplistic ankle, you can now confidently show the world your beautiful anklet. Just by its looks, it is guaranteed high quality and durable.

Conclusion

Wow that was a really enjoyable learning journey and we hope that you have learned a lot from all those projects and looking forward to your beautiful creations!

But before we part ways, I would like to give you a piece of advice regarding wire jewelry making, always remember that you must love what you are doing and have lots of practice and perseverance because it will make you master the craft easily!

Wire Jewelry for Beginners:

Super Detailed Guide To Make Your Own Wire Jewelry In No Time!

Introduction:

Since childhood women love jewelry, but they always need to wait till the men are going to give it to them. Instead, why don't you try yourself in a new hobby and fill the box with your own handmade jewelry! Apart from jewelry, all the women are into creativity. So, it is a great idea to demonstrate your creative skills, choose color and mood, bring your image to perfection, add a playful touch or try on the veil of mystery. Such magnificent purpose can be achieved without buying expensive accessories and fashionable haute couture clothes.

Moreover, it is enough to master making jewelry with your own hands. Women have the right to choose in jewelry sophistication or simplicity, modesty or showiness, but one should not forget that jewelry has its own symbols. Particularly, it is a direct reflection of your taste. That is why homemade jewelry will always be a win-win.

Women's hobbies are interesting and diverse; in most cases they are also useful. Needlework is probably one of the most prominent examples, especially when it comes to making handmade jewelry. Necklace looks amazing along with the dress, bracelet will definitely suit your new bag and earrings should be in harmony with the individual style!

No one else will be able to limit the creative flight and fantasy by a meager assortment. It's not just about the perfect complement. In no case should one lose sight of the price: neither with the purchase nor with the manufacture. Perhaps one of the main advantages of this unusual hobby is the ability to independently choose the value of the product. This is justified by the fact that nowhere can one meet such a rich choice as in stores specializing in the "assembly" of jewelry.

You can find various details, consult a specialist, pick up what you are looking for and find new ideas. However, it does not mean that the components can be found exclusively there. Old beads, an exclusive stone, which could not be used by any means, and long torn chains, as well as rhinestones, rings, ribbons and threads, can gain a new life! You just need to experiment and turn on the imagination.

Chapter 1 – How to start working with wire jewelry

If you are interested in making jewelry as a hobby, you do not need to be a professional. Kits for making jewelry will bring you main materials and tools to do everything without any assistance. There is one more pleasant surprise you might find in such a kit.

It is instruction that also contains a great deal of ideas, however, if you are fed up with copying somebody's creativity, trust your own imagination. Jewelry kits could be different, as they take into consideration all your preferences.

For example, you might opt for beadwork jewelry sets, stuffing jewelry sets and wire jewelry sets, etc. It is enough to remember the main tools, such as clamp and scissors. Special pliers (or clamp) come in handy to compress and decompress the rings without any problems. These very rings (from 2 to 5 millimeters in diameter) serve to connect parts, for example, pendant and chain, chain and clasp.

Scissors are always used for their intended purpose to give the necessary length of tape, thread, fishing line, wire or chain. We never forget that we should first measure out seven times, and only then cut them off! And then you can act on intuition - the assembly of jewelry is in many ways similar to the designer. Everything is in your arms.

The task is a little more complicated when the necessary components need to be done personally. For such purposes, often use polymer clay, from which you can make anything - flowers, emoticons, letters and various shapes. In the process, it resembles plasticine, and, when frozen, becomes like plastic. After that, the part you made can be used as a pendant or keychain. However, such a thing can come up with an infinite number of applications.

In addition to the assembly, there are interesting jewelry making techniques. Thus, the Shambhala bracelets that have become a hit in recent years can be performed only if you know the basics of macrame. Weaving beads is always useful, especially if you prefer or would like to work with fishing line.

It means that for this type of creativity one does not need to possess any special aptitude. It is enough to possess knowledge that you have in the scope of applied art, and if you do not have it, fantasy is the main tool. Also, ideas for costume jewelry with your own hands can be drawn from online photos or magazines.

Felting in the creation of jewelry is most often used in the form of soft colored balls, which can be the main elements of a necklace or bracelet, giving them a special lightness. Stylish bracelets and other jewelry made of genuine leather are always in fashion, for which old leather things can be used, and a thin cord soutache technique.

Select the specific jewelry project and think if you are eager to create unforgettable earrings, charming bracelets or sophisticated necklaces. The next step is to find out all appropriate material, for instance, you might as well work with beads, paper, wire, and resin.

If you don't have any ideas what to do, look though numerous websites or go to the local shop, and you will return totally inspired. After you have defined the primary idea, think about the main tools you will need for work:

- ✓ *Various flat nose pliers are divided into several categories, such as roun, chain, flat, curved and nylon ones;*
- ✓ *Wire cutters;*

✓   *Wire to create the basis of jewelry;*
✓   *Wire bending pag boards.*
✓   *Metal ruler.*

Though handmade jewelry is about your flow of imagination, we should outline key accessories you will never live without. Indeed, jewelry kit is a good option to choose as they have already had all the necessary things, but the jewelry might seem quite similar, afterwards. So, if you want to be different, regard what you need exactly and buy it.

As well, you need to calculate and measure a lot if you want to present such jewelry as a gift. It is not always comfortable to ask about the size, that's why masters usually orient on some standards acceptable in this business. The samples might look differently as it depends whether you have prepared it for girl or boy.

The next point to consider is the length of necklaces. As there are a lot of them in the industry, measure system also varies from one to another example. For instance, the length of chokers is 38 cm, rope necklaces are nearly 86 cm while princess-style necklaces are approximately 45 cm.

If you pay attention to the necklaces that are worn on the collar, their length is 17 inches (if it is designed for women) and 50 cm (in case their owner is man). The total length of the bracelets is about 18 cm for women and from 25 cm for men.

Chapter 2 – The main skills you will need to work with wire jewelry

To create your own jewelry, you had better be aware of main skills and approaches. They include making hoop rings, cutting wire, wiring, cutting and using tools and a peg, etc. Concerning the hoop rings, different workshops allow creating a ring with a stone suitable for both beginners and those who already have ideas about jewelry. At this step, you need to learn how to melt the metal on your own, solder the base for the ring, fix the stone and process the finished jewelry.

The insert can be selected from the proposed collection of precious and semi-precious materials or bring your own stone. *The advantage of aluminum wire* is its low price. Its main disadvantages are:

- Low resistance to bending - in order for the wire to break, it suffices to bend it sharply only a few times;
- Aluminum oxides do not conduct well, and it oxidizes very quickly;
- Significantly lower electrical conductivity - with the same thickness, aluminum wires withstand less stress than copper.

The undoubted advantages of copper wire are:

- High resistance to mechanical stress - copper wire can be bent and twisted for a rather long time without any damage to its integrity;

- Copper is less oxidized, but even its oxides are electrically conductive;

- The high flexibility of the copper wire makes it easier to install and reinstall sockets and switches. Here you do not risk the fact that as a result of careless movement of the wire coming out of the wall, will break in the most inconvenient place.

- Copper conducts electricity noticeably better than aluminum.
- Copper has one and only disadvantage, particularly, a higher price.

When you are ruled by the desire to take up your jewelry business, follow the guidelines you have purchased which are about to illustrate all the steps of jewelry crafts. Once you opted for jewelry, practical wire represents a great tool to practice accessories making and only after that you have enough skills to spend money on more expensive items.

Thus, you will be able to hone your skills with a large number of repetitions, and finally you will be convinced that your jewelry has appeared to become better.

Chapter 3 – How to produce earrings

Do you like **Swarovski**? Perhaps, you have already got some jewelry as the present from your beloved and dearest people… But if you want to become a master, the best thing to start is from **crystals earrings.** They will look fantastic, and do not require excessive efforts to complete.

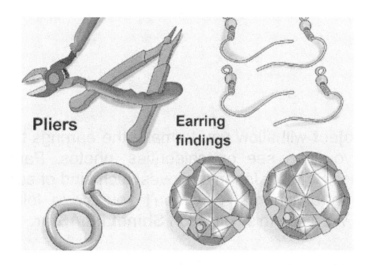

Pliers   Earring
                findings

It is quite easy to make such earrings and they need a couple of crystals, two hopping rings and a pair of earring pins. Next, good pliers will do you a favor to bend the jewelry in the right places.

Use the pliers to flip and open two rings. Bring the crystals on from the ring. Stay convinced that once the crystals possess clear sides, both front and back, the upper side is to be demonstrated in front, as soon as you close the ring. As soon as the crystals appear on the race rings, put the earrings onto the ring. Use pliers in order to lock the jewelry item.

The next project will allow you to make the earrings that resemble the jewelry you can see on celebrities' photos. Particularly, the famous actress Scarlett Johanson loves such kind of earrings. If you are a true fan of cinema, why don't you try to follow the next instructions? We'll call this collection **ShineLikeAStar.**

These earrings will require such tools as tuler, round-nose pliers, side cutters, platypus, file and two pliers. Wire thickness is 1.0 cm, 0.8 cm, 0.6 cm. Also, you will need not too large chain, four glass beads of blue color in the form of a drop, four suspensions also in the form of a droplet.

For the fasteners you need to cut side cutters 2 pieces long by 8 cm from a wire 1.0 mm. Use a file to finish the tips so as not to scratch your ears. Pliers round curl a loop. "Platypus" hold the loop bending the wire. Make two identical spirals with tails of 4.5 cm each. Next, wrap both our arms around the auxiliary tool (it can be a knob from a crochet hook with diameter of 0.6 - 0.7 cm.) Round pliers slightly bend the ends.

This is what you are going to receive as the result:

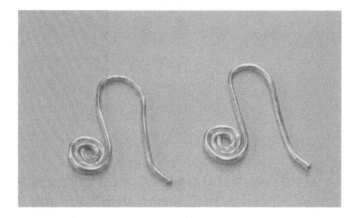

Cut 15 cm of wire with a thickness of 0.6 cm. Screw on a stick or toothpick. Dissolve the spiral. From such a twisted wire form a ball, so that it could not fall apart the free end several times pass through the future bead.

Align with pliers so that the bead could become round.

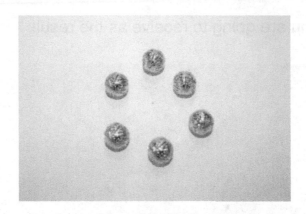

Make a ring on which will hang a glass bead and suspension. Cut 12 cm of wire with a thickness of 0.8 cm. Wind around a round object (here a bottle of ink) with a diameter of more than 1.0 cm. Leave one end longer. Into the ring, thread the bead and the pendant. Hold the long end of the wire with pliers, wind the short with 2-3 times, cut off the excess. Put the bead-ball on the rod. With the help of round pliers, make a loop.

Make four blocks like that:

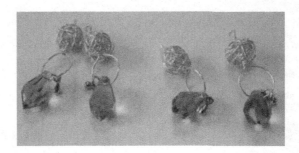

Next you need to make 2 oval rings. Wire 1.0 cm wound on the tip of the "platypus", cut the excess with side cutters. Attach, passing through the center, to the oval ring bolts. Disconnect 12 links from the chain. Attach the fifth link to the ring fastener. At the ends of the chain, unclip the links, attach the beads from the wire. Attach

81

another piece of 4 links to the bead on a short chain. And now to the free ends of the chains, extending the links, attach the block.

The earrings are ready:

From the wire with the effect of memory, you can come up with a lot of ideas for assembling earrings with your own hands. So, we will tell you in detail about how to **make earrings with your own hands using wire memory**, along with amethyst beads and chains.

Fittings:

Memory wire - 2 turns

10mm amethyst beads - 24pcs

Glass beads - 4 pieces

Metal beads - 2 pieces

Snowflakes - 4 pcs
Earrings-1 pair
Chain - 30 cm

Tools:

✓   *side cutters, pliers*

We cut off three segments from the whole chain. Each segment should be slightly longer than the previous one. For example: 5 cm, 6 cm and 7 cm. On the edge of the first twisted ring we form a loop with round pliers. String accessories on the wire in the sequence as in the photo:

Repeat the pattern on the other side connecting the remaining edges of the chains parallel to each other. We'll form a loop at the end of the wire and connect them with a clip. Let's make in the same way the second earring. Instead of round beads, you can use crumb or any other beads, depending on the desired material.

Chapter 4 – How to produce bracelets

The popularity of bracelets made of stone beads of various shapes is quite understandable. Firstly, polished natural stones are beautiful, presented in a variety of color variations, including shades, overflow, moire patterns, crystal clarity or rich color fullness. Secondly, this entire range is available to the buyer along with the most intricate accessories for jewelry, various inserts, pendants, dividers and latches. All that is necessary, you can choose in the shops for needlework, at gem fairs, in online stores.

Thirdly, making bracelets from natural stone is an occupation that does not require special knowledge or skills, you need only desire and a little time. Fourthly, you can create jewelry from stone beads according to your wishes, choosing the desired color and shape, in accordance with the outfits and costumes. As we see, there are enough advantages, it remains only to find out how these decorations are made. The work starts with the selection of beads and accessories for the composition.

Beads are not only of a different color, but also of a different texture (matte, glossy, transparent, translucent, opaque, colored, with the effect of crackelure, etc.), of different cut, of different shapes, of different sizes. The finished bracelet will look more interesting if you use spectacular combinations of different beads and accessories in its manufacture. First of all, **to create the bracelet**, we will use natural agate beads, the smallest (0.4 cm) - white agate, medium (0.5 cm) - black agate, large (0.8 cm) - dragon vein coloring agate.In addition to these, hollow metal openwork beads of silver color are useful.

Locks for our bracelets are not necessary, because the elastic thread spandex will allow putting on a bracelet without unbuttoning. We measure 20 -25 cm of thread, at the end we tie up a reliable large knot so that the beads do not roll off on the other side in the planning process.

Tying a knot on a spandex can be a difficult task, the thread will tend to straighten up. In this case, you can attach a stationery clip to the tail. Then we begin to string the beads on a string in the chosen sequence, and the scheme of stones can be either symmetrical or not.

One metal bead in our agate bracelet has become a dotted shiny accent. When you get enough beads, just in case try on the length of your wrist, complete the bracelet. Pull off the spandex and tie on a strong triple knot. Trim the tips to the very knot, otherwise they will hang up ugly. Tighten the knot inside any beads.

Similar bracelets can be made from a variety of stones: rock crystal, jasper, tourmaline, coral, charoite, hematite, turquoise, aventurine, onyx and others.

In order to make bracelets in the second project we propose, we need ordinary manicure or simple scissors, round-nose pliers and pliers to manipulate the ringlet. The next is beads. You might take white sugar quartz. The beads are different in diameter, but it seems that it will turn out to be a good combination. Also, we need a rubber thread, of which there are also a lot in the hardware stores. It is of different thickness, but you had better take at least 0.7, what is less likely to tear.

You still need a needle, the eye of which will miss the gum. This is to make the gum double, but it is not necessary. You also need to take this into account when choosing stones. The neo-beads have very narrow, so there is no way to hold a rubber band, not to mention a double elastic band.

Therefore, pay attention to the fact that in the beads the holes are wide enough for a needle and a double thread. Three details, a ring, a bale and a butterfly, are necessary in order to decorate the second bracelet. Bead-dividers and dividers are needed to make the bracelet interesting and unusual. Pay attention to a large bead with a large hole, usually a knot is hidden under such a bead.

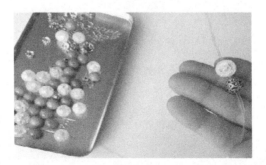

Now we start to make a bracelet. First, measure the girth of the arm and cut as much thread as is enough with a large margin on your wrist. Measure immediately with the thread in the needle. After all, you need a double thread.

It is important to wear the largest bead in order to hide the knot at the very end. Then it all depends on your imagination, what bead shapes you want, color, and what dividers you are willing to have. These are simple dividers and bead caps, you can use dividing beads. Key moment in the bracelet is node. We tie, as usual, and make the usual double knot. We still have four such threads after tying a double knot.

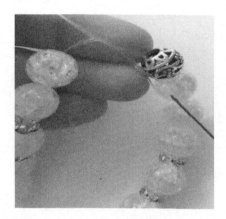

These four threads need to be wrapped and passed through their own ring, which was formed. And tighten firmly until it stops, pulling in two directions in two threads. Afterwards, pull the gum under the big bead and hide the knot.

There are a number of jewelry, particularly, bracelets that can be worn for both men and women. The scheme of **weaving Shambala bracelet** is simple, even a beginner can master it. As a result, you get a stylish decoration.

Women of the fair sex can also wear it, but for this purpose, appropriate materials should be selected. This product is a wreath of special square knots and large beads. Before creating it, let's define the history. Shambhala is a non-existent country in the mountains of Tibet, which is described in many legends and tales not only of the peoples of Asia, but also of the indigenous people of Altai.

It is believed that the first bracelets were worn by Tibetan monks; they were woven into a cord with beads, precious stones, and gems. Such an amulet reliably protected its owner from the evil eye, poison, evil thoughts and enemies.

In the modern fashion industry, this bracelet was introduced by two brothers: Mads and Mikel Cornerap. Since 1994, such jewelry made of precious metals and stones began to be produced under their trademark. The brothers in their collections combined the folk art of Scandinavians, Asians, yoga practice and Indian symbolism.

To make a Shambala bracelet, we will need the following materials:
- ✓ *Waxed rope. Instead, you can take a strong braid, micro cord, synthetic or leather cord*
- ✓ *Colored beads or stones*
- ✓ *Thread for stringing beads (needed if you have a large braid)*
- ✓ *Clasp*

As well, you will need such tools as scissors; lighter; ruler; scotch; needle; and glue.

The scheme is the following:

- Take 3 laces approximately 50 cm long each. They may not necessarily be plain, you can take different colors.
- Put the laces together and tie them in a loose knot (we will untie it later) at a distance of 5 cm from the edge.
- We put the leftmost cord on top of the central one.
- We put the extreme right on top of the left, which is located on the center. We stretch its edge under the lower (central) and draw the end into the loop, which was formed between the left and central cord.
- Tighten the side threads.
- Ensure that the central nodule is always straight.
- Now we begin to weave the second bundle: the principle of "vice versa" is in effect. That thread that was left, we have become on the right side, and vice versa.
- Put the left thread under the center.
- You put the right one under the left one and the end over the central one.
- Stretch cords - knot number two is ready!

The classical scheme implies one row of beads. For this:

- Weave 4-5 knots.
- In the 6th knot, a bead or a stone should be strung on the central thread, and the knot should be completed, like the previous ones.
- Further in all knots weave your decorative elements - beads, pebbles.

- Finish the decoration with knots. Their number should be the same as at the beginning.

- Now we make the lock. To do this, flip the bracelet, tie the left and right thread with a normal knot. Tighten well and treat the plexus with glue. Wait for it to dry well.

- Cut tails. And so that they do not fluff, burn them with a lighter. Repeat the procedure on the second edge of the bracelet.

Chapter 5 – How to create a necklace

Every girl wants to stand out. The unique jewelry is intended to help in it, especially when it comes down to the creation of necklace.

To make beaded necklace, take:
- ✓ *large beads with a diameter of about 1.5 cm;*
- ✓ *chain with large links - about 45 cm;*
- ✓ *pins-guides - 1 pack;*
- ✓ *transparent beads;*
- ✓ *decorative fastener;*
- ✓ *connecting rings - 2 pcs .;*
- ✓ *pliers and round pliers.*

Choose a color palette yourself, but we recommend you to take beads to match. The combination of pearl beads and Czech beads No. 10 looks beautiful. As for the number of beads and studs, it depends on how voluminous you want to see the finished decoration.

The necklace is made like this:

- We string a pin on a pin-carnation, and a bead behind it.
- We act in the same way with all the drivers that are decided to use.
- Bend the ends of the pin-studs around the links of the chain in several rows.
- Attach the clasp with a connecting ring.
- The second ring is attached to the opposite edge of the chain.

The advantage of this decoration is that it is easy to change, disassemble and reassemble. If the beads are rubbed, you can always replace them with new ones or add necklaces of other shades. Next, to make the following necklace from the colorful beads, you will need other tools.

✓   *decorative caps - 2 pcs .;*
✓   *round fastener - 1 piece;*
✓   *multi-colored beads with a diameter of 1 cm;*
✓   *0.8 cm beads of different colors;*

✓   *jewelry cable - 4 m.*

✓   *side cutters and pliers.*

The toggle has the form of a circle and sticks, which is passed through it. This is a popular type of furniture, decorating the finished work.

Here's how to do motley jewelry on your own:

- Measure out 1 m cable in folded form.
- We pass the cable through a part of the castle and measure out the middle of it.
- Fasten the fastener in the middle of the cable with a stub and pliers.
- String a bead with a diameter of 1 cm and fasten it with a cable at the fastener.
- On the sides we strung on the bead and fasten both of them, pulling the cable through them.
- We string and fasten another bead - a cruciform pattern is formed.
- We continue to weave to the desired length and fasten the second part of the fastener.
- Weave a row of beads with a size of 0.8 cm.
- We interweave both rows of the necklace with the remnants of a cable and tie a strong knot.

Choosing the color of beads, pay attention to their location in the weaving. Most beautiful is a necklace with a clear alternation of shades or a pronounced gradient transition from tone to tone. The decoration made by your own hands will be the subject of your pride and envy of those around you.The realization that no one else has such an accessory is worth the effort spent on making a unique necklace.

To make **a necklace of satin ribbons** with your own hands, prepare the following materials:

✓   2 pieces of ribbon of two colors (preferably contrasting) 0.7 cm wide;

✓   sharp scissors;

✓   glue;

✓   lighter or matches;

✓   2 pin-carnation;

✓   2 embosser for beads;

✓   2 large beads;

✓   a trailer for a chain with a fastener.

Materials will require a minimum, but as a result you will create something incredibly beautiful and original. So, how to do it step by step:

- Fold each tape in half, slightly press on the fold to outline the middle.

- On the fold line of one tape drip a little glue and glue the second tape on top, placing it perpendicular to the first.

- It turned out cruciform billet. Dry it well to fix the decoration base.

- Bottom tail tape, located vertically, flip up through the second tape, leaving a small loop at the bottom. Press the connection point with your fingers.

- Throw the top tail of the same ribbon down, leaving a loop of the same size. Press your fingers.

- You will have two loops resembling a bow.

- Pass the left tail of the ribbon horizontally into the top loop.

- Pass the right tail of the same ribbon to the bottom loop.

- Tighten the knot loosely. Then the final drawing will be beautiful and voluminous.

- You get a square shape knot.

- Continue to weave the knots until you reach the desired length of the necklace.

- Make sure the tapes fit flat. Align them if necessary. So you will timely eliminate the resulting folds or misalignments.

- The result is a beautiful three-dimensional base.

- When finished weaving, trim the ends of the ribbon. Take sharp scissors, so the material will not push.

- The edges of the tape sing with a cigarette lighter.

- Fold them together and alternately glue on top of the last knot.

- The base for the necklace is ready. Now make a convenient fastener.

- Pass the pin-stud through the last knot so that the sharp part becomes a kind of continuation of the blank.

- Similarly, decorate the second end of the necklace.

- Put on each pin a bead-hugger, covering the ends of the necklace with a "hat".

- Put the pin-stud on top of the big ball.

- Bend the pin in the ring. If necessary, "bite off" the excess length with scissors so that the loop is not too large.

- Hide the tip of the pin inside the hole in the bead.

- From the remnants of the tape make a clasp. Cut the ribbons into two identical pieces.

- Depending on the length of the tape, adjust the length of the decoration.

- Thread each pin into the loop. Edge singe a cigarette lighter or matches.

- Fix the ends with a fastener along the edges of the ribbons, pressing them as tightly as possible.

Conclusion

Accessories in creating a fashionable image can make wonders. Lovely baubles in the form of jewelry interestingly beat even the most unsightly outfit and make a woman a gorgeous lady, seductive beauty or tender girl.

Appropriate and well-chosen accessories are the final touch of a stylish ensemble. Moreover, it is not necessary to buy jewelry in the finished form, as a necklace, earrings or bracelets made on your own will look especially nice and unforgettable.

Made in United States
North Haven, CT
07 January 2024

47133833R10070